JAPAN

ABDO
Publishing Company

JAPAN

by A. M. Buckley

Content Consultant
Hiroshi Ono
Associate Professor, Texas A&M University, Department of Sociology

CREDITS

Published by ABDO Publishing Company, 8000 West 78th Street, Edina, Minnesota 55439. Copyright © 2012 by Abdo Consulting Group, Inc. International copyrights reserved in all countries. No part of this book may be reproduced in any form without written permission from the publisher. The Essential Library™ is a trademark and logo of ABDO Publishing Company.

Printed in the United States of America,
North Mankato, Minnesota
062011
092011

♻ THIS BOOK CONTAINS AT LEAST 10% RECYCLED MATERIALS.

Editor: Melissa York
Copy Editor: Susan M. Freese
Design and production: Emily Love

About the Author: A. M. Buckley is an artist, writer, and children's book author based in Los Angeles, California. She has written several books for children.

Library of Congress Cataloging-in-Publication Data
Buckley, A. M., 1968-
 Japan / by A.M. Buckley.
    p. cm. -- (Countries of the world)
 Includes bibliographical references and index.
 ISBN 978-1-61783-115-7
 1. Japan--Juvenile literature. 1. Title.
 DS806.B77 2012
 952--dc22
                              2011007736

Cover: Japan's Mount Fuji

TABLE OF CONTENTS

CHAPTER 1
A VISIT TO JAPAN

As you sail into the harbor of the largest metropolitan area in the world, you marvel at the serene view of a mist-shrouded Mount Fuji in the distance beyond the city. Back home, you practiced using chopsticks and watched anime cartoons, but you know that these are only small elements of Japanese culture. What will it be like—this island nation with a history that stretches back nearly 40,000 years?

NAKAJIMA TEAHOUSE

The Sumida River trip leaves from the Hama Detached Palace Garden, a 62-acre (25-ha) garden originally built in 1654.[1] Like many historic sites in Tokyo, the palace and surrounding trees and vegetation were destroyed during World War II, but they have all been restored. The palace, built in a traditional Japanese style, appears to float on the pond like a mirage. When US President Ulysses S. Grant visited Emperor Meiji of Japan in 1879, the two leaders shared tea at the old Nakajima Teahouse on the palace grounds.

The Rainbow Bridge stretches across Tokyo Bay. The bridge is actually white, but at night it is illuminated by multicolored lights.

IMPERIAL PALACE

Construction on the Imperial Palace began in 1590, when Japan's first shogun set to work building the world's biggest castle. Only the inner circle remains in the center of Tokyo today, but much of the castle has been rebuilt. It is here that the emperor, the symbolic head of Japan, lives with his family.

Before you can guess, the smiling attendants efficiently guide you and the other passengers off the ship.

There are so many treasures to see in Tokyo that it's hard to know where to begin. To get your bearings, you take the Sumida River trip. Following the Sumida River through the city, the trip takes you from central to northern Tokyo. Awaiting the next boat, you sip green tea while you look out over the beautifully restored palace and carefully tended garden in the historic garden and teahouse of the Hama Detached Palace Garden.

As you board the tour boat, you see the blue waters sparkle, reflecting the glittering skyscrapers along the shore. The boat moves into the salt water of Tokyo Bay and back up the river, passing beneath 12 bridges, each whimsically painted a different color. You pass by some of the thousands of Japanese islands, including Tsukuda, a lively fishing village and a center of the famous Edo-era culture. One of the few areas of Tokyo that escaped destruction during World War II (1939–1945), the sixteenth-century buildings here are like living pieces of history.

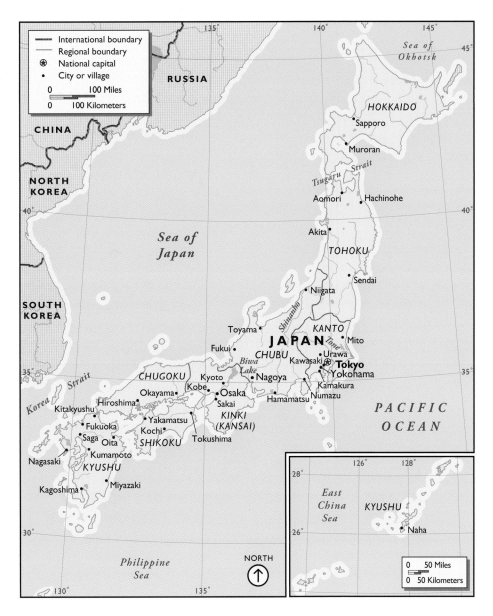

Political Boundaries of Japan

TOKYO TOWER

At 1,093 feet (333 m), Tokyo Tower is even taller than the monument that inspired it, the Eiffel Tower in Paris. Since it was built in 1958, Tokyo's monument has been the tallest self-supporting steel structure in the world. It is painted bright orange and white so pilots will be able to see it from the air. Tokyo Tower is lit with 176 floodlights and shines orange during winter and white during summer.[2]

As you make your way up the river toward northern Tokyo, you enjoy the view of the contemporary city skyline. You spot glimpses of the Imperial Palace and the glamorous shops of Ginza, one of many famous shopping districts in Tokyo.

You don't want to miss Tokyo Tower in Shiba Park. You ride the elevator to one of two observation decks to take in a panoramic view of Tokyo and, because it's a clear day, you gaze at Mount Fuji rising above the surrounding lakes in the distance.

You get off the boat in northern Tokyo, which is a haven of Shinto shrines, Buddhist temples, and historic museums. Wander through the spacious Ueno Park and Zoo to see animals from around the world and to marvel at the seventeenth-century five-story pagoda.

Though it's growing late, you let the energy of the local people inspire you, and you hop on a subway to Shibuya in western Tokyo. You're among more than 2 million people that pass through Shinjuku Station most days. In addition to shoppers and teens, you know thousands of Japanese businesspeople travel this route to work long hours in the city's many modern office buildings.[3]

But Shinjuku is not all work. Not far from the bustle of the station is Harajuku, where Japanese teens come to shop for their diverse and outrageous fashions. Nestled among high-fashion shops and an antiques market, you find a shrine to Admiral Togo, who led Japanese naval troops to victory over Russia in 1905. As the day winds down toward

Tokyo Tower is somewhat reminiscent of the Eiffel Tower in Paris, France.

evening, you pop into a restaurant where lively groups are enjoying one of Japan's favorite national pastimes, karaoke.

BALANCING OPPOSITES

All across Tokyo, historic shrines and pagodas mingle with gleaming new office buildings and museums, visual proof of Japan's blending of opposites: old and new, East and West, secular and religious, work and play. You're just as likely to see sandaled monks in orange robes as orange-haired teens in sky-high platform shoes, women in traditional kimonos as in designer suits, rushing businesspeople on cell phones as elderly couples strolling in the park. It's this embracing of difference and love of change that makes Japan so distinct.

Japan has 15 million cell phones, the seventh most in the world.

Japan's history stretches back so far that pottery found in ancient Japan is the oldest-known clayware in the world. For centuries, Japan isolated itself in this island home, fostering a unique culture and lifestyle. Upon the insistence of a US naval officer, the nation reconnected with the world in 1854. After the fall of Japan's last shogun, or leader of its military dynasty, in 1867, the nation gradually embraced Western-style democracy. After opening to the world, the Japanese set out on an expansionist drive that led to wars with its neighbors and land disputes that remain undecided even today.

The people of Japan celebrate the old while embracing the new.

Elements of Japan's long and ambitious cultural, religious, and political history are apparent in everyday life. Historic victories and crushing defeats are evident in the many monuments and shrines to leaders and in the once-ruined structures that have been carefully restored.

Bright signs catch shoppers' attention in Tokyo's busy streets.

As you saw in Tokyo's museums and shops, the Japanese enthusiastically participate in traditional arts and culture, such as the tea ceremony and flower arranging. Even so, they are also eager to participate in all things new, including technology, art, fashion, and more. Japan's comfortable balance of ancient traditions and modern culture can be seen in day-to-day life throughout the nation.

SNAPSHOT

Official name: Japan (Japanese: Nihon or Nippon)

Capital city: Tokyo

Form of government: parliamentary democracy with a constitutional monarchy

Title of leader: prime minister (head of government); emperor (head of state)

Currency: yen

Population (July 2011 est.): 126,475,664
World rank: 10

Size: 145,914 square miles (377,915 sq km)
World rank: 61

Language: Japanese

Official religion: none

Per capita GDP (2010, US dollars): $34,200
World rank: 39

CHAPTER 2
GEOGRAPHY: AN ISLAND NATION

The nation of Japan consists of a chain of approximately 3,900 islands lying along the Pacific Rim of the continent of Asia. The islands stretch in a 1,500-mile (2,400-km) arc between the Pacific Ocean to the east and the Sea of Japan to the west.[1] Japan's four main islands—Hokkaido, Honshu, Shikoku, and Kyushu—make up 97 percent of its 145,914 square miles (377,915 sq km) of territory. In all, Japan is slightly smaller than California.

The area that is now Japan was originally connected to the continent of Asia by a land bridge called the Tsushima Strait. That area separated into islands at the end of the last Ice Age, approximately 10,000 years ago, when the narrow strip of connecting land was covered over by water.

Japan is located at the intersection of four tectonic plates, which makes it one of the areas of greatest geologic activity in the world. The

Picturesque Mount Fuji is an active volcano.

International boundary
National capital
City

0 100 Miles
0 100 Kilometers

Cropland
Pasture
Forest

RUSSIA

CHINA

NORTH
KOREA

SOUTH
KOREA

Sea of
Okhotsk

Kuril
Islands

Asahi Mtn.

Hokkaido

Sapporo

Hakodate

Tsugaru Strait

Sea of
Japan

Sendai

Honshu

JAPAN

Shinano

Japanese Alps

Watarase

Tone

Fukui

Kawasaki

Tokyo

Sumida
Tsukuda

Mount Fuji

Kyoto

Nagoya

Yokohama

Kobe

Biwa
Lake

Osaka

Hiroshima

PACIFIC
OCEAN

Izu
Islands

Kitakyushu

Korea Strait

Shikoku

Fukuoka

Nagasaki

Kyushu

Philippine
Sea

NORTH

East
China
Sea

Ryukyu Islands

Okinawa

Naha

0 50 Miles
0 50 Kilometers

Geography of Japan

nation has approximately 1,000 minor earthquakes a year and has experienced several severe earthquakes. After an earthquake, tsunamis may also strike Japan.

Approximately 80 percent of Japan's land is mountainous, and at least 100 of the nation's mountains are active volcanoes.[2] Japan's most famous natural monument, the graceful and symmetrical Mount Fuji on the Pacific coast on Honshu, is the tallest mountain in Japan. Fuji remains an active volcano.

Japan's many mountains are also home to clear lakes, bamboo groves, thick forests, and cherry trees. Each spring, the cherry trees blossom all across the country in waves of pink and white.

The same geothermal activity that causes volcanic eruptions and earthquakes is responsible for hot springs, naturally forming pools of water heated by the earth. There are more hot springs in Japan than anywhere else on the planet.

EARTHQUAKES

Japan has seen more than its share of disastrous earthquakes. One of the worst earthquakes hit the cities of Tokyo and Yokohama on September 1, 1923, killing at least 100,000 people.[3] In 1948, the small city of Fukui was nearly destroyed by a massive earthquake. In January 1995, another huge earthquake struck the city of Kobe, killing more than 5,000 people.[4] On March 11, 2011, a 9.0-magnitude earthquake hit Japan, the largest quake recorded in the country's history. The quake triggered a tsunami that devastated the coast of Honshu, killing thousands and making at least 320,000 people homeless.[5]

Japan is located in eastern Asia. Its closest neighbors are Korea to the west, Russia to the northwest, and China to the southwest. The relatively isolated nation stretches from the island of Hokkaido in the northeast to the Ryukyu Islands in the southwest.

Off the western coast of Honshu lie the Ryukyu Islands, a cluster of 65 islands. The most visited of these is Okinawa, and the entire area is often referred to by that name. To the north are the Kuril Islands, once part of Japan but part of Russia since World War II. Japan has long attempted to regain these northern islands.

Japanese hot springs are called _onsen_.

HOT SPRINGS

Japan's thousands of hot springs lend a steamy haze to the landscape. In addition, the springs have provided its citizens with a unique bathing and relaxation experience for centuries. Referred to as _onsen_, the hot springs are popular destinations throughout Japan.

Some onsen are located near the sea and accessible only when the tide is out. Others are nestled along fast-running streams or waterfalls in the mountains. A number of onsen are located in the cold, hilly region of Hokkaido, and some require more than a day's walk to reach. The smaller islands, too, have their share of onsen.

The Japanese enjoy onsen vacations, and locals and travelers alike can book rooms in a _ryokan_, a special type of lodging found near some hot springs. There, guests can lounge in their rooms or bathe in the springs at their leisure. In addition to the onsen's relaxing qualities, these waters have healing properties, according to the Japanese.

AVERAGE TEMPERATURES AND RAINFALL

Island (City)	Average January Temperature Minimum/Maximum	Average July Temperature Minimum/Maximum	Average Rainfall January/July
Hokkaido (Hakodate)	19/32°F (-7/0°C)	61/73°F (16/23°C)	2.6/5.4 inches (6.6/13.7 cm)
Kyushu (Nagasaki)	36/48°F (2/9°C)	73/84°F (23/29°C)	2.8/10.1 inches (7.1/25.7 cm)
Honshu (Tokyo)	28/46°F (-2/8°C)	70/82°F (21/28°C)	1.9/5.6 inches (4.8/14.2 cm)[6]

CLIMATE

Japan's climate varies by region. The northernmost island of Hokkaido is cool, with cold and snowy winters. The other three biggest islands—Honshu, Shikoku, and Kyushu—are temperate and rainy, with warm summers and cool winters. The summer is rainy overall. The Pacific coast is also rainy in the fall, and the coast of the Sea of Japan is also rainy in the winter. The Ryukyu Islands have a more subtropical climate. They are warm year-round, with hot summers. The rainy season there starts in May and moves northward, ending in late July. Another natural phenomenon common to Japan is typhoons. These large, hurricane-like storms strike each year in late summer or early autumn.

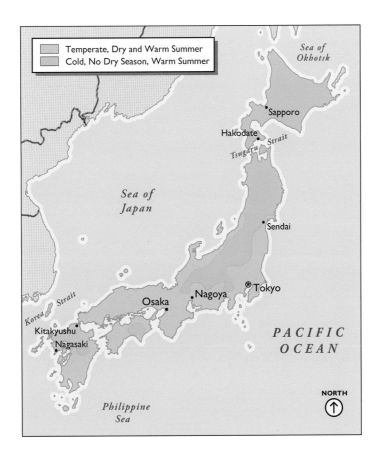

| Temperate, Dry and Warm Summer |
| Cold, No Dry Season, Warm Summer |

Sea of Okhotsk

Sapporo

Hakodate

Tsugaru Strait

Sea of Japan

Sendai

⊛ Tokyo

Nagoya

Osaka

Korea Strait

Kitakyushu

Nagasaki

PACIFIC OCEAN

Philippine Sea

NORTH ↑

Climate of Japan

MOUNTAINS, CITIES, AND COASTS

Japan's moist climate has created a fertile, green interior, with thick forests, bamboo groves, lakes, and natural hot springs. But because

the land is so mountainous, less than 15 percent of it can be used for agriculture.[7] Clever farmers have cultivated the green valleys and used terraces to grow rice and other crops on steeper slopes.

Japan's highest mountain ranges, located in central and northern Honshu, are known collectively as the Japanese Alps. The eastern side of the Alps, which borders the Pacific Ocean, is more highly populated and well traveled. The western side is less populated and not traveled as often, earning it the nickname *Ura Nihon,* or the "backside of Japan." The Japanese Alps played host to the 1998 Winter Olympic Games, which took place in Nagano. Japan also hosted the 1972 Winter Olympics in Sapporo on the island of Hokkaido.

REGIONS AND PREFECTURES

Japan's islands are divided into eight main regions: Hokkaido, Tohoku (northern Honshu), Kanto (includes Tokyo and Yokohama), Chubu (central Honshu), Kinki/Kansai, Chugoku, Shikoku, and Kyushu (includes Okinawa). These eight regions are politically organized into 47 prefectures, each of which has its own capital city, legislative assembly, and governor or executive.

Along the coasts, the mountains dip into low-lying plains. These have been highly developed into large metropolitan areas. There are

Japanese farmers make terraced fields on hillsides to use as much land for agriculture as possible.

three main urban areas: the Nagoya complex, the densely populated Tokyo/Yokohama, and the large Kobe/Kyoto/Osaka industrial complex.

The Ryukyu Islands are graced with white sand beaches and coral reefs. Only a short boat ride from Taiwan to the south, these islands have a geography and climate more similar to southeast Asia or Hawaii than mainland Japan.

Nippon, the Japanese word for "Japan," is often translated as "land of the rising sun."

Snorkelers enjoy the clear blue waters off Okinawa in the Ryukyu Islands.

CHAPTER 3

ANIMALS AND NATURE: AN ENVIRONMENT AT RISK

From the snowy peaks of Hokkaido to the steaming jungles of Okinawa and throughout the lush, green valleys in between, Japan is home to a variety of animals. Many of these animals are similar to those found in China and Korea. They arrived on the islands centuries ago, crossing the land bridge that once connected Japan to Asia. However, a number of animals and birds are endemic to the islands, found nowhere else.

Of the 94 mammal species found in Japan, 46 are exclusive to the island nation.[1] These include the Japanese dormouse, found on Honshu and Shikoku, and the Ryukyu long-tailed giant rat, found on Okinawa and the Ryukyu Islands. The Japanese macaque, also known as the snow monkey, lives on Honshu, Shikoku, Kyushu, and some of the smaller

Japanese macaques are known to bathe in hot springs.

islands. Another animal unique to the islands is the Japanese giant salamander, found in western Honshu and on Kyushu. On average, this massive reptile weighs 55 pounds (25 kg) and is approximately 5 feet (1.5 m) long.

Some animals endemic to Japan are becoming endangered. For example, the Iriomote cat is a small, very rare cat that is considered to be a prehistoric animal. But today, no more than 100 of these cats still exist. Another animal that is endemic to Japan but increasingly rare is the Amami rabbit, a small, short-eared rabbit. Only approximately 2,500 of these animals remain today.[2]

Other mammals in Japan include boars, deer, and bears. Brown bears are found in the north on Hokkaido, and Asiatic brown bears are found on the other islands.

Approximately 370 species of birds are found in Japan, but unlike the mammals, most of these species are not native to Japan.[3] One endemic bird that has fared better than some mammals is the Okinawa woodpecker. It was near extinction in the 1930s but is recovering now thanks to efforts to save it.

The rivers, lakes, and seas of Japan are home to many kinds of water birds and fish. The birds include a variety of cranes, such as the red-crowned crane. This long-legged black-and-white bird, with red on

A brown bear in Hokkaido catches a fish.

top of its head, is found on Hokkaido. Another water bird is the white-naped crane, a grey species with red around its eyes, which winters on Kyushu.

In the waters of Japan are approximately 200 species of freshwater fish; about 50 of these species are endemic.[4] In addition, there are a number of saltwater fishes in the oceans surrounding the island nation.

Like the animals, many of the fish in Japan are endangered. At particular risk are several types of tuna, which have been fished in large amounts for sushi and other popular dishes. To help save the tuna, especially the bluefin tuna, international regulations limit how many can be fished.

Several species of whales pass through Japanese waters, including blue whales, fin whales, minke whales, and humpback whales.

ANCIENT FISH

There are more varieties of primitive fish found in Japan than in any other area of the world. Five types of lampreys and four types of sturgeons come from ancient lineages.

Whale meat is found in some Japanese restaurants and markets.

Japanese red-crowned cranes dance in the snow in Hokkaido.

PLANTS FROM AFAR

The plants of Japan vary by region. On Hokkaido, the forest includes fir, spruce, and pine trees. Okinawa and the southern islands have a subtropical forest with broadleaf evergreen trees. Plants that live in alpine regions thrive in the higher areas of Honshu and Shikoku, and forests of beech trees can be found throughout many regions of Japan.

Many of the plant species in Japan have been introduced to the area over the years. Out of approximately 5,600 plant species, about one-third

NATION'S GAIN IS NATURE'S LOSS

Mining was one of the earliest sources of environmental damage and pollution in Japan. During the late 1800s, copper was one of Japan's main exports, and 40 percent of it came from the Ashio Copper Mine, located in Tochigi prefecture. This mine was operated by the Furukawa Company from 1878 until it was closed in 1973.

During the years the Ashio Copper Mine operated, it caused significant environmental damage. Thousands of acres of forests were destroyed in the operation of the mine, and the polluted water it created ruined crops in the area. This water also flowed into the nearby Watarase River, killing many fish and causing serious health damage to the people who lived along the river.

The copper seam in the mine was finally depleted in 1973, and the mine was closed. But using ore from other sources, area refineries continued to operate until the early 1980s. Significant efforts have since been made to restore the land and water around the mine, but it will take many years and more effort for the environment to recover fully.

Japan is famous for the cherry trees that blossom each spring.

are endemic to the area.[5] Between 200 and 500 of these plants were introduced from North America and Europe in the late nineteenth and early twentieth centuries.[6]

Some of the favorite plants in Japan are endemic to the islands. These include a large, blue-purple flower called shirane-aoi and a rare plant with light-purple flowers found high in the mountains in Honshu, the togakushisgouma. A type of rare grass found in the rocky mountains of Japan, urahagusa, is popular in home gardens and potted plants.

WASTE LAWS AND WATER BOTTLES

With so many people living on islands and in densely packed cities, waste management and recycling are of particular concern in Japan. The Japanese government has put in place complex laws that have reduced the waste that people throw away. Today, the average Japanese household throws away half as much as the average US household. However, the Japanese have two problematic sources of waste: They use billions of pairs of disposable wooden chopsticks, and they sell water and other drinks in plastic bottles and cans in their 5.5 million vending machines.[7]

NATURE UNDER THREAT

Japan is not a large nation in size. Nevertheless, it has developed into one of the world's economic superpowers through its rapid industrialization. The downside of this economic growth has been a severe depletion of Japan's beautiful natural beaches, mountains, and forests. As the cities have expanded, these natural habitats have disappeared or been polluted with chemical fertilizers and pesticides for farming. A number of Japan's animals, plants, birds, and other forms of life have become extinct. In the past 150 years, the Japanese wolf, the Japanese sea lion, the flying fox, and more than a dozen birds have become extinct. More than 300 animals are in critical danger of extinction.[8]

It has become clear in recent years that Japan's rapid industrialization and stunning success in technology and industry have taken a serious toll on the environment. The threats include deforestation, pollution, urban and commercial development, and commercial farming.

ENDANGERED SPECIES IN JAPAN

According to the International Union for Conservation of Nature (IUCN), Japan is home to the following numbers of species that are categorized by the organization as Critically Endangered, Endangered, or Vulnerable:

Mammals	28
Birds	40
Reptiles	12
Amphibians	19
Fishes	59
Mollusks	25
Other Invertebrates	132
Plants	15
Total	330[9]

In addition to cutting down forests for timber and mining the mountains for valuable minerals, the Japanese have had to shore up their fragile environment to build the large urban centers where so many of them live. As a result, beaches, rivers, and other natural areas all over Japan have been reinforced by cement supports, further encroaching on nature and animal habitats.

In the past decades, Japan has taken a great interest in protecting the environment. In 1997, the country hosted the meetings where the world's leaders met to create the Kyoto Protocol, an environmental treaty that calls on all nations to curb greenhouse gas emissions. Japan has some of the world's strictest environmental regulations, including the Nature Conservation Act of 1972. Two government agencies—the Ministry of Agriculture, Forestry, and Fisheries and the Agency for Cultural Affairs—have the power to designate special natural areas as cultural landmarks. Receiving this designation provides federal protection for the area and guides the government to create laws to protect nature.

Japan is the world's largest importer of coal.

Since increasing its awareness of conservation in the 1970s, Japan has established 29 *kokuritsu koen*, or "national parks." In addition, there are 56 parks called *kokutei koen*. Although these are not official preservations,

Many Japanese waterways are edged with concrete, reshaping the original habitats.

designating them as parks has aided in conserving the environment. The total area of both types of parks makes up less than 1 percent of Japan's land. However, approximately 14 percent of Japan is under protection of the government or protected privately in some fashion.[10]

Zao Quasi National Park protects this volcanic crater and its distinctive green lake.

CHAPTER 4

HISTORY: A LEGACY OF ADAPTATION

Evidence has shown that humans have lived in the area that is now Japan for at least 200,000 years, although the first archeological artifacts from the area date back to 35,000 BCE. Experts believe these early people arrived on land bridges that once connected Japan to China, Korea, and Siberia.

By about 13,000 BCE, a hunter-gatherer society called the Jomon had formed in Japan. Their pottery and stone tools are among the oldest human artifacts in the world today. The Jomon are the ancestors of the Ainu, a small group of indigenous people still living in Japan today.

The Ainu consider Mount Fuji sacred.

This terracotta figure dates to the Jomon period.

EARLY HISTORY BOOKS

A number of books were written under Emperor Temmu during the Yamato era. These books detail events from Japan's mythic past. Titles include *Kojiki* (The Record of Old Things), from the year 712, and *Nihon Shoki* (The Record of Japan), from the year 720. The imperial family used these semihistorical books to establish its claim to divine rule.

Amaterasu means "shining heaven."

New migrants continued to arrive from Asia and spread north from Kyushu to Hokkaido. Their presence pushed the natives farther north. By about 330 BCE, these arrivals had established an agricultural society known as the Yayoi. They used sophisticated wet rice-farming techniques and made tools from iron and bronze. The Yayoi society established a series of kingdoms. By the middle of the third century CE, a queen named Himiko ruled over all of these kingdoms. After she died, the Yayoi established a royal line of emperors that were said to have descended from the sun goddess Amaterasu. That line of royalty continues to this day.

The Yayoi period was followed by the approximately 700-year dynasty of the Yamato family, known as the Kofun or Yamato era. During this time, Japan's leaders saw China as a nation of strength and wealth and decided to emulate Chinese policies. The Japanese adopted Buddhism, a Chinese import from India, and a Confucian-influenced government. In the year 604 CE, a constitution was established, and by 645 CE, Japan had a centralized government and system of law inspired by China.

Japan was ruled by family dynasties for several centuries. The Nara and Heian periods, each led by a different ruling family, followed the Yamato period. But for one family to stay in power, it had to prevent certain members and rival clans from holding important positions. Doing so led to jealousy and infighting.

During the Golden Age of the Heian, from the ninth to the twelfth centuries, the arts flourished at the imperial court of Kyoto. At the same time, leaders outside Kyoto used their military might to vie for power. Far from the peaceful and artistic capital, a class of warriors known as samurai began to gather strength.

SAMURAI

Samurai began as farmer-warriors who were employed by the Japanese emperor. During the twelfth century, the samurai continually gained power, until the Kamakara shogunate took over as the first samurai-influenced government. The samurai soon became the highest nobles.

The samurai code of ethics, Bushido, emphasized endurance, whole-hearted commitment, and sincerity. The code had a strong influence on Japanese culture. Over time, the samurai shifted from warriors to aristocrats, but they remained powerful through the middle of the nineteenth century. Numerous books and movies have memorialized the brave and powerful Japanese samurai.

THE RISE OF
THE SHOGUNATE

Two rival families of noble samurais, the Taira and the Minamoto, emerged as the strongest, but the Minamoto eventually prevailed. In 1192, Minamoto Yoritomo overtook the throne. He chose, however, not to be the emperor but rather a shogun, or military leader. This ushered in a period of military rule that would last approximately 700 years. The emperor remained in Kyoto, but the shogun effectively ran the government from his base at Kamakura.

During the rule of the Kamakura shogunate, Japan successfully fought off two invasions by the Mongols, who ruled much of Asia. The first attack came from Korea in 1274, and the second came from China

KAMIKAZE

During the second Mongol invasion of Japan, in the year 1281, the word *kamikaze*, or "divine wind," was used to describe the typhoon that destroyed many of the invaders' ships. Many believed divine intervention had helped Japan beat the invaders.

During World War II, the word *kamikaze* was used to refer to Japanese pilots who deliberately crashed their planes into Allied warships. Because the planes were usually loaded with explosives and full of fuel, they became like missiles when crashed into ships.

At the Aoi festival in Kyoto, historical reenactors wear clothes from the Heian era during a ceremonial procession.

in 1281. Both times, the invaders met with strong resistance from Japanese warriors, and when they returned to their ships for reinforcements, the invaders were vanquished by massive storms. The few that survived turned back.

When the shogun Minamoto Yoritomo died in 1199, his widow, Masako, controlled the shogunate for the remainder of her life. She established her own family, the Hojo, as the new line of rulers. Her family ruled until the powerful Ashikaga family seized power in 1333. The Ashikaga shogunate reestablished the capital at Kyoto and again emphasized the arts, such as the tea ceremony and theater. This began a combative era of regional conflicts, looming civil war, and the arrival of Europeans.

In 1543, shipwrecked Portuguese sailors arrived in Japan. These sailors were the first Europeans to arrive in Japan, and they introduced guns and Christianity to the islands. In 1568, Japanese military leader Oda Nobunaga used the new firearms successfully to seize control of the capital of Kyoto. He first installed one of the Ashigawa clan as shogun but soon took over himself. He ruled until 1582, when he was betrayed by one of his own generals. Both Oda Nobunaga and his successor used their power to unify Japan's warring provinces into one strong nation.

Masako was called the *ama*, or "nun," shogun.

A wood-block print depicting a samurai in battle from the Edo period

In 1603, the Tokugawa shogunate took over a unified nation with the goal of maintaining power and order. They established the capital at Edo (which is today Tokyo) and instituted strict control. Japanese society was divided into four classes: the samurai at the top, followed by farmers, artisans, and then merchants. People were not allowed to shift from one class to another, and laws were enforced harshly. The Tokugawa shogunate instituted a policy of *sakoku*, or isolation, turning away or executing foreigners who came to Japan. This shogunate ruled for 250 years in a period that would become known as the Tokugawa or Edo period. During this isolated era, Japanese culture flourished.

From 1635 to 1853, only the Dutch and Chinese were allowed to trade in Japan.

A MODERN JAPAN

Japanese culture and society changed in 1853 with the arrival of US Navy Commodore Matthew Perry. The United States did not want to conquer Japan; rather, US military might forced Japan to open itself to foreign trade. The Japanese did not have modern guns to defeat the US arrivals. The shogunate suffered a humiliation that signaled the beginning of the end of its long rule.

From 1867 to 1868, a group of Japanese reformers wanted to end the shogunate's military rule of the country and reinstall the

US Navy officer Matthew Perry met with Japanese leaders in 1853.

emperor as the true leader. Led by samurai from the south and the west, they took over the military government in a coup called the Meiji Restoration. The city of Edo was renamed Tokyo, which became the new base of the restored imperial government.

RICH COUNTRY, STRONG ARMY

The Meiji government had two primary slogans. One was *oitsuke, oikose*, which meant "catch up, overtake," and the other was *fukoku kyohei*, which meant "rich country, strong army." Both slogans accurately represented Japan during an era of growth and imperialism.[1]

Emperor Mutsuhito, later called Meiji, ruled from 1868 to 1912 in a period of intense growth and development. Much as Japan had looked to China for inspiration in earlier centuries, it now looked to the West as a new power to imitate and perhaps surpass. A parliamentary government was put in place, although the emperor still remained at the head of the government. The class system was dissolved, and Western-style banking, railways, and clothing were introduced. The government also developed its military, growing into a power to rival the United States and Russia.

By the late 1800s, Japan had begun a series of military missions to expand its territory. Japan entered Korea in 1876 and intervened in that nation's government for several years. In 1894, Japan started a war

Emperor Meiji, *center*, and the imperial family, ca. 1900

with China. Japan won easily and took over the Liaotung Peninsula.
From 1904 to 1905, Japan was at war with Russia, ultimately beating
the much larger nation and emerging as a new world power. Japan
then invaded and took over Korea, ruling it from 1910 to 1945. Tension

Emperor Hirohito ruled Japan during World War II.

between the two countries persisted for much of the post–World War II period.

By the early twentieth century, Japan had become a power in the region, but a variety of factors had greatly diminished its admiration of the West. One of these factors was a 1924 US immigration policy that limited how many Japanese could move to the United States.

EMPEROR OF THE SUN

Emperor Hirohito was the one hundred twenty-fourth emperor of Japan. Ruling from 1926 to 1989, he led the nation during nearly seven decades of tumultuous wars that included stunning victories and crushing defeats. Emperor Hirohito was the longest-ruling emperor in the history of Japan. Japan remains the nation with the world's oldest hereditary monarchy, or unbroken line of rulers from a single family.

In 1926, Emperor Hirohito took the throne of Japan, and he ruled the nation until his death in 1989. Hirohito established the period referred to as *Showa*, which means "illustrious peace." Despite the name, Japan continued to invade its neighbors, including Manchuria in 1931 and China in 1937.

Germany invaded Poland in 1939, touching off World War II. Japan joined forces with Germany and the other Axis powers, contributing its considerable military might to their war effort. Most notably, Japan bombed the US naval base at Pearl Harbor, Hawaii, in 1941, which prompted the United States to join the war. Japan fought hard but surrendered after US forces firebombed Tokyo and dropped atomic

bombs on the cities of Hiroshima and Nagasaki.

Following the end of World War II, the United States occupied Japan. The Americans did not depose the emperor, who remained on the throne. However, they drafted a new constitution with a policy that prohibited Japan from building an active military or going to war. Japan allowed democracy, and by 1952, the United States left Japan to independent rule. (The United States remained on the island of Okinawa, where there was a military base, through 1972.)

The second half of the twentieth century was a period of growth and

A nuclear bomb devastated the city of Hiroshima in 1945.

ATOMIC BOMBS

World War II ended in the Pacific when the United States dropped two atomic bombs on Japan, forcing the nation's surrender. This was the first and only time nuclear weapons were used against people in the history of the world.

The first bomb was dropped on the city of Hiroshima on August 6, 1945. The bomb was said to have more than 2,000 times the power of the world's next most destructive bomb. A US plane dropped the bomb on Hiroshima, a city with a population of 318,000.[2] Nearly one-third of the city's residents—90,000 people—were killed in the blast.[3]

Only three days later, on August 9, 1945, US and Allied forces dropped a second atomic bomb on Japan. The target of this bomb was the city of Nagasaki. Of the city's 174,000 residents, 22,000 died on the first day and another 17,000 died within four months due to catastrophic injuries suffered from the blast.[4] The radiation and other effects of the bombings are still felt by the inhabitants of these cities.

On August 14, 1945, Emperor Hirohito accepted US terms, and on September 2 he formally surrendered the nation. Japan came under US rule through 1952.

change for Japan. Their military might curtailed, the Japanese went to work rebuilding their economy. The tradition of nationalism continued but was expressed in new ways. Participation in the new democracy was widespread, and people took it upon themselves to rebuild their nation's strength through economic power. As the nation grew richer, cities were transformed into modern economic hubs. The construction business was booming, creating new industrial complexes as well as residential developments. Within a few short decades, the island nation had transformed into a major economic powerhouse.

By the 1990s, what had been referred to as Japan's economic miracle began to dissolve. The nation was beset with a massive recession. Many workers lost their jobs as the Japanese currency lost value. The 1990s have since been referred to as Japan's Lost Decade.

The economy began to recover at the turn of the twentieth century but struggled, like other nations, in the global recession late in the decade.

On March 11, 2011, the largest quake in Japanese history struck the island nation. Centered near Sendai, a city on the northeast coast of Honshu Island, the quake was felt strongly in Tokyo and even further away. The quake and the resulting tsunami flattened homes and cities along the coast. A month later, almost a million homes were still without power. By June, the count of dead and missing had climbed to 24,000.[5]

In addition, damage to nuclear power plants caused the worst nuclear disaster in the world since the Chernobyl accident in the Soviet Union in 1986. One plant suffered a partial meltdown, and a second plant

The March 11 earthquake and tsunami destroyed large regions of Japan's coast.

began to release radioactive material into the air. Months after the quake, the nuclear reactors were not yet completely contained.

CHAPTER 5

PEOPLE: TRADITIONAL LIVING

As of July 2011, Japan had a population of 126,475,664—the tenth-largest population of all the countries in the world.[1] Before World War II, most Japanese lived in farming villages. However, since the war, Japan has undergone a rapid transformation to industrialization, and more and more people have moved into cities to work in manufacturing jobs and corporations.

LANGUAGE AND WRITING

The national language is Japanese. About half of Japanese words are of native Japanese origin. Approximately 40 percent came from Chinese, and the rest were derived from English and other European languages.[2] Many of these words are different in Japanese, however. For example, the English word "juice" is *juuse* in Japanese. Manners, including the use of the

Women celebrate Mother's Day with a fan dance.

Japanese writing is formed with characters.

correct and polite words and expressions, are very important to Japanese culture, and this is reflected in the language.

Writing has been integral to Japanese history for centuries, both as an art form and a means of communication. Written Japanese is not formed with letters but instead consists of symbols called characters.

These characters were brought to Japan from China approximately 1,500 years ago. Japanese can be written using three different systems of characters, called kanji, hiragana, and katakana. Kanji is the most complex and formal system, while hiragana, also called kana, is the simplest and most widely used. Traditional Japanese is written vertically—from the top of the page to the bottom—in columns starting on the right. A more modern way of writing Japanese mimics the left-to-right horizontal rows of English.

Calligraphy, a flowing style of writing characters that is similar to painting, has been highly valued in Japanese culture for centuries. Children

THE LANGUAGE OF MANNERS

The Japanese language reflects the importance of respect. There are a variety of ways of saying *you* and *I*, depending on who is speaking and who is being addressed. Children are addressed using informal language but speak formally to adults. Also, it is considered impolite to address a person using the incorrect form for his or her age or status. Likewise, it is considered impolite to be too forthright or to communicate negative opinions directly. Subtlety is valued.

In addition to spoken language, body language is used to communicate both respect and humility. The most prominent form of body language is the bow, used commonly throughout Japan. Somewhat like a handshake in American culture, a bow is used as a greeting, but there are different forms for various circumstances.

A variety of social norms, or rules, govern the practice of bowing. For example, men bow with their hands at their sides, and women bow with their hands touching lightly in front of them. The heels are kept together in a proper bow, and the degree of bend in the body communicates the form of the bow and the relationship between the two people. The deeper the bow, the more respect it communicates.

study calligraphy in school. A number of Japanese schoolchildren also learn English, which is a challenge because English differs significantly from Japanese in its pronunciation and alphabet.

THE JAPANESE PEOPLE

The Japanese belong almost entirely to a single ethnic group: 98.5 percent are Japanese. Another 0.5 percent are Korean and 0.4 percent are Chinese, while 0.6 percent of the people derive from other ethnic groups.[3] One of these groups is Ainu, an indigenous Japanese ethnicity.

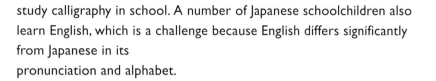

AINU AND BURAKUMIN

Most Japanese have the same ethnic heritage, but two minority groups—the Ainu and the Burakumin—have historically faced discrimination. The Ainu are indigenous to Japan, but they were steadily forced northward throughout history and now reside mainly on the northern island of Hokkaido. Burakumin are people who have Japanese ancestry, but their ancestors worked in professions considered unclean by the Buddhist majority because workers had to touch blood or dead bodies (such as butchers, leather workers, and grave diggers). The government has outlawed discrimination against the Burakumin, but they are sometimes treated unfairly in marriages and employment.

Ethnic Ainu in Hokkaido celebrate their heritage.

Due to tight regulations on immigration, approximately 2.2 million foreigners live in Japan, which is only 1.7 percent of the total population.[4] Most of these individuals are from Korea, China, and Taiwan. A significant number also come from Brazil, and a few come from the United States.

The Japanese have a life expectancy of 82.25 years, among the highest life expectancies in the world. But today's aging population is a concern for Japan. The median age is 44.8 years old, and 64 percent of Japanese are between the ages of 15 and 64. Close to 23 percent of Japan's citizens are 65 or older, while only 13.1 percent are children aged 0 to 14.[5]

In addition to the issue of an aging population, Japan faces the issue of a shrinking population. The average birth rate is only 1.2 children per woman. According to predictions, if this trend continues, Japan's population will shrink to 100 million by the year 2050.[6]

The average Japanese person lives almost four years longer than an American.

RELIGION AND NATURE

There is no official national religion in Japan, but a large percentage of Japanese practice Shintoism, a religion native to Japan, and Buddhism, a religion native to India. Both religions are devoted to nature and find beauty in the natural cycles of transformation. Shintoism is practiced by 83.9 percent of Japanese and Buddhism by 71.4 percent. The overlap between these numbers reflects how the two religions are practiced side

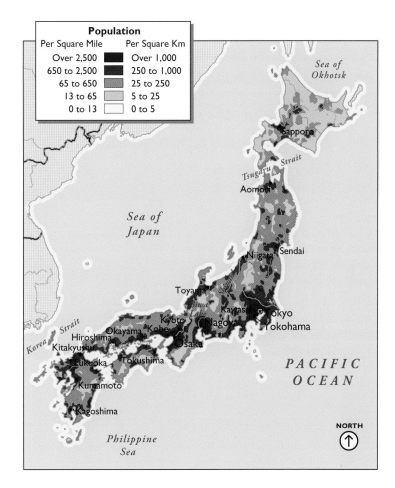

Population

Per Square Mile		Per Square Km
Over 2,500		Over 1,000
650 to 2,500		250 to 1,000
65 to 650		25 to 250
13 to 65		5 to 25
0 to 13		0 to 5

Sea of Okhotsk

Sapporo

Tsugaru Strait

Aomori

Sea of Japan

Niigata Sendai

Toyama

Kawasaki Tokyo
Kyoto Nagoya Yokohama
Okayama Kobe
Hiroshima Osaka
Kitakyushu
Fukuoka Tokushima
Kumamoto

Kagoshima

PACIFIC OCEAN

Philippine Sea

NORTH
↑

Population Density of Japan

by side. Two percent of Japanese practice Christianity, and 7.8 percent practice other religions.[7]

The word *Shinto* means the "Way of the Kami."[8] The Shinto religion is based on the idea that all things in nature are animated by a *kami*, or spirit. These things are worshipped in nature and in shrines called *jinga* or *jingu*. A rope near a river or tree signifies that it is sacred. Shinto rituals use simple materials, such as paper fortunes and smoky incense. The entrance to a Shinto shrine is marked with a *torii*, a special door or gate. The torii consists of two beams topped by two horizontal pieces—the top one curved. Worshipers wash their hands and mouths before entering.

SHINTO SHRINES

The Shinto religion dictates that each shrine be taken down and rebuilt every 20 years on a nearby site. The shrine must be built using the original plan and building style, using interlocking joints instead of nails. The wood from the original shrine is used to make the *torii*, or gate, on the new shrine.

Japan's most sacred Shinto shrine, Ise-jingu, is located in Ise in the Kansai region and dates back to the third century. This shrine was rebuilt in 1993, and the shrine's newest incarnation has a rebuild date of 2013. Ise-jingu is dedicated to Amaterasu, the sun goddess, from whom Japanese emperors are believed to descend.

Buddhism began in India and arrived in Japan from China in the sixth or seventh century. It was integrated into Japanese culture and has been a significant part of the nation for centuries. Buddhists accept and value change, which is ongoing in life. Buddhist temples have a clean, simple look, which has influenced Japanese art forms. The altar may be graced

Shinto shrine in Kyoto

YOU SAY IT!

English	Japanese
Hello	Konnichiwa (kohn-nee-chee-WAH)
How are you?	O-genki desu ka? (oh-GEHN-kee dehss-KAH)
My name is _____.	Watashi no namae wa _____ desu. (wah-TAH-shee noh nah-mah-eh wah _____ dehss.)
Nice to meet you.	Hajimemashite. (hah-jee-meh-MAHSH-teh)
Please	Onegai shimasu (oh-neh-gah-ee shee-mahss)
Thank you	Domo arigato (doh-moh ah-ree-GAH-toh)
You're welcome	Do itashi mashite (doh EE-tah-shee mah-shee-teh)
Yes	Hai (HEYE)
Excuse me	Sumimasen (soo-mee-mah-sehn)
I'm sorry	Gomen-nasai (goh-mehn-nah-seye)

with a flower or rock. The primary form of Buddhism in Japan is Zen Buddhism, which focuses on austerity and mental control.

Because many Japanese practice both the Shinto and Buddhist religions, it is not uncommon to see two altars in a contemporary Japanese home. The religions share an understanding and acceptance of transience, or the fleeting nature of life, and an appreciation for nature. These values can be seen in the widespread observation and celebration of brief but beautiful natural events, such as the blossoming of the cherry trees and the changing phases of the moon. The Japanese tend

In Japan, many people practice Buddhism along with Shintoism.

to consider Shinto, with its gods of nature, to be a religion for life on Earth and Buddhism, with its influence on the passing nature of all things, to be a religion that addresses the afterlife.

Christianity came to Japan with the first Europeans in the sixteenth century. It was not hugely popular, but some Japanese converted. Because of an uprising generated by Christians, the shogunate killed a great many people of this faith in 1638. For many years after that, Christians in Japan practiced in secret. Today, the country's constitution protects individuals' freedom of religion.

CHAPTER 6
CULTURE: AESTHETICS AND INNOVATION

The Japanese people, as a whole, are devoted to hard work and family values but also make time for fun and celebrations. Aesthetics, leisure, religion, and education are all important to the Japanese.

The family—the cornerstone of Japanese society—is traditionally patriarchal, with the father working and the mother taking care of the household. Traditionally, an aging parent also lives with the family, but this is not always the norm in contemporary Japan. Increasingly, women work outside the home and men make more time for their families.

Elements of Buddhism and Shintoism, the two primary religions, influence the culture. This can be seen in the Japanese appreciation for nature and respect for the cycles of life. Leisure activities outdoors include picnics and travel, particularly to natural hot springs and beaches.

Traditional arts and practices such as the tea ceremony are still celebrated today.

FLOATS AND PROCESSIONS

Some Japanese festivals are celebrated with elaborate floats, costumes, puppets, and figures. For example, Nebuta Matsuri, held from August 2 through 7, features magnificent floats and huge paper lanterns. At the end of the festival, the floats and lanterns are traditionally carried out to sea, symbolizing the release of anything that might interfere with the season's harvest. During Aoi Matsuri, celebrated on May 15 in Kyoto, people wear costumes from the sixth century Heian period. They walk from the palace to the shrines in a re-creation of an imperial procession meant to placate the gods.

The Japanese also celebrate *matsuri,* or "festivals," throughout the year. Shinto or Buddhist traditions or nature itself inspire the majority of these festivals. For example, each spring when the cherry trees bloom, the Japanese have parties outdoors. Soon afterward, during Golden Week from April 29 through May 5, the Japanese take time off to travel. The Japanese celebrate Buddha's birthday nationwide on April 8, and they visit shrines and temples in celebration of the New Year on January 1. The emperor's birthday is also celebrated as a national holiday.

Sumo wrestling, the informal national sport of Japan, evolved out of ancient Shinto prayer rituals. Sumo rituals include clapping, stomping, and throwing salt on the mat before a match. Popular Western sports include

Sumo wrestlers face off at a tournament in Fukowa.

soccer and baseball. Japan has had a baseball league since 1934 and has produced a number of world-class players. In recent years, many Japanese baseball players, including Hideki Matsui and Ichiro Suzuki, have gone to play for professional US teams. Soccer is also important in Japan, and the nation cohosted the World Cup with Korea in 2002.

Some popular activities in Japan include dining out, traveling, singing karaoke, playing board games, and attending festivals. Leisure pastimes include reading—everything from comics called manga to a variety of literature and poetry—and an extremely popular pinball game called *pachinko*. Bathing in public baths is another traditionally popular pastime.

As a culture, the Japanese value the group over the individual. Participation in family life and community groups, such as close groups of classmates and work associations, is an important part of Japanese culture.

The Japanese value hard work, but they like

SAVING FACE

In Japan, the concept of saving face relates to maintaining the dignity and honor of one's status or position. It is important to respect one's boss, teacher, or elder and to keep relations harmonious. A child's misbehavior reflects as poorly on the parents as the child. Socially and in business, it is generally considered impolite to say no or to express a negative opinion, so polite Japanese people find a way around it. For example, a businessperson may nod politely to acknowledge a proposal even if it is being rejected.

to have fun, too. Alcohol consumption is popular, and it is common for business colleagues to gather for drinks in bars after a long workday. Karaoke—perhaps the most popular national pastime—is also enjoyed in restaurants and bars all over Japan.

THE BEAUTY OF EVERYDAY LIFE

Aesthetics have long been valued in Japanese culture, and daily life is infused with elements of beauty and creativity. The Japanese have developed writing, gardening, and simple activities such as storing food and wrapping gifts into forms of art. Food, clothing, gifts, packaging, and decor provide an opportunity to present something in a visually appealing way. Even an everyday packet of gum or a book of matches comes in a clever package, in which every detail—from the design to the illustration and colors—has been carefully selected. This awareness prevails in food and clothing as well.

Lunches may be packed in neat containers called bento boxes, and sushi may be tied with a seaweed ribbon. Food is picked up and eaten with chopsticks, which are utensils made of long, thin pieces of wood or plastic. Beautiful gardens are cultivated in graceful designs. Ikebana, the art of flower arranging, began in the sixteenth century and continues to be popular in Japan today. Calligraphy has also been important to Japanese art and culture for centuries. The graceful lettering, which appears on

In Japanese, chopsticks are called *hashi*.

painted screens and in books and scrolls, takes great patience to learn.

Today, a majority of Japanese wear Western-style clothing for work and school but dress in traditional clothes for ceremonies and special occasions. Jeans and dresses are common, and among Japanese businesspeople, the dark suit is the norm. Students and many company workers wear uniforms.

Despite the popularity of Western-style dress, traditional Japanese clothing is not out of place even in urban centers. A traditional garment for both men and women is the kimono, a dress with wide sleeves and, for women, tied with an obi, or wide sash. The variety of styles of kimonos can vary widely, from a lightweight summer kimono to a heavily embroidered silk dress kimono.

Women in kimonos practice the art of ikebana.

PACKAGING GIFTS

Twice a year, the Japanese offer gifts to friends, family, and coworkers to express their appreciation. *Ochugen* gifts are given around midsummer, and *oseibo* gifts are given in December. These gifts are carefully chosen and wrapped. In gratitude, it is common for the recipient to write a thank-you note or to give a *temiyage*, a gift given in thanks for a present. Boxes and packages, once carefully wrapped in fabric or with artfully placed twine or functional and beautiful netting, are now sold in stylish commercial packages. But when given as gifts, these too are now wrapped in beautiful decorative paper.

EATING SIMPLY

Kome, or rice, is a staple of the Japanese diet and is served with nearly every meal. The most prevalent kind is white rice called *hakumai*, often served steamed. Less common is *genmai*, an unpolished brown rice found mostly in Buddhist temples and organic restaurants. Rice is also made into soup, rice balls, and sushi, one of Japan's most famous cuisines. Sushi is a rice dish flavored with vinegar, often including raw seafood and vegetables.

Slurping noodles is good manners but burping is rude in Japan.

Noodles are also popular in Japan. Some common types are udon, which are thick noodles made from wheat flour, and soba, which are thick noodles made from buckwheat. Ramen, which originated in China, is also prevalent in Japan. Noodles are served with meat or vegetables or in soups.

Seafood is another staple in the Japanese diet. It is served in a variety of ways, including raw, grilled, fried, dried, prepared into cakes or balls, or made into paste for soup. Tofu, a soybean curd popular with vegetarians the world over, is also found in many Japanese dishes. Tofu is often served cold, topped with ginger and onion. Tofu can also be fried in sesame oil or included in soups. Salty miso paste, made from fermented soybeans, is a popular condiment and soup ingredient. Another Japanese condiment served with

Sushi is carefully prepared to be decorative as well as delicious.

TEA CEREMONY

Tea was initially brought to Japan from China sometime during the seventh or eighth century. Tea was very popular but rare, so it was reserved mostly for priests and nobles. A specialized art form called the tea ceremony evolved around the drinking of tea. The formal tea ceremony dates back to the sixteenth century and was developed in the imperial court and in Buddhist religious ceremonies.

Over the centuries, the tea ceremony grew and flourished into a form of fine art. Today, many Japanese still partake in the tea ceremony. Every element of the ceremony is planned and designed for maximum beauty, elegance, and grace. Specialized utensils include a scoop for the tea, called a *chashaku*; a *chasen*, or bamboo whisk, used to whip the green tea into a froth; and *chawan*, which are bowls or cups from which to drink the tea. Everything about the tea ceremony—including the table setting, the view through the windows, and the accompanying sweet—is carefully chosen and patiently appreciated.

many dishes is shoyu, or soy sauce. This flavorful brown sauce substitutes for salt in most Japanese foods.

A typical Japanese meal contains rice topped with vegetables and fish or meat cooked with soy sauce, a bowl of miso soup made from soybean paste, and a dish of *tsukemono*, or pickles.

Tea is the main drink of Japan and has been the centerpiece of elaborate ceremonies for centuries. The Japanese drink alcohol at many festivals and special occasions and also for relaxation after work. Sake, a rice wine that can be served warm or cold, is a traditional drink that is still enjoyed today. However, beer has become more popular. Snacks served with drinks at bars include sushi and *yakitori*, which are skewers of grilled chicken and vegetables.

Japanese meals sometimes end with fruit, but sweets are served on special occasions and with ceremonies. Japanese *okashi-ya*, or sweet shops, sell a wide variety of sweets, and many include a red bean paste called *anko*.

THE FLOATING WORLD

Traditional Japanese aesthetics are based on the principles of harmony and balance with a subdued and elegant style. The beauty of incongruity, or the unexpected, is also appreciated. Since the creation of the earliest ceramics in the Jomon period, the visual arts have flourished in Japan. These include many types of ceramics, painting, and printmaking, as well as arts unique to Japan, such as ikebana, lacquerware, and, more recently, anime, or animation.

Karaoke is a shortened form of *kara okesutora*, Japanese for "empty orchestra."

Japan has an extensive and distinctive art history that intertwines with and breaks off from traditions in the West and other Asian nations. One example of this is ukiyo-e, which translates as "pictures of the floating world." These woodblock prints were made in Japan from the seventeenth through the nineteenth centuries and depict scenes of daily life and pleasurable events, such as beautiful landscapes and entertainers. In Japan,

these prints were mass produced and were intended to be as fleeting as the subjects they depicted. But in Europe, they became popular and were collected and saved.

Lacquerware, which is made by painting an object with multiple layers of lacquer to achieve a deep gloss, also became popular around the world. Given the Japanese preference for subtle beauty, the most common colors of lacquer are dark brown and black. These colors reflect light in deep and subtle layers, rather than as a bright shine.

Contemporary Japanese artists are influenced by Western art forms as much as their own history. Perhaps the most famous Japanese artist in the world today is Takashi Murakami, whose work has been included in important museums in Japan, Europe, and the United States. His work embraces mass production and includes paintings, sculptures, and performances, as well as factory-made watches, shirts, toys, and purses.

The earliest geisha were men, entertainers similar to European court jesters.

FROM GEISHA TO J-POP

Japanese music also has traditional and contemporary strains. Traditional music is influenced by music and instruments from China. The Japanese *koto*, or lute, originated

Manga is a popular Japanese style of art.

in the country and is the national instrument. Since the Meiji Restoration, Western-style music and dance have taken hold, and the Japanese have produced their own styles and stars based on rock and pop music traditions.

Traditional theater reflects the Japanese interest in subtle beauty. The classic Noh theater, dating back to the fourteenth century, has an austere look and hypnotic music. It is performed on a spare stage by two principal dancers and musicians.

Kabuki and bunraku were developed by the merchant class during the seventeenth century. At the time, merchants were considered the lowest class of people and not very important. As such, they were less subject to the strict laws of the era. The merchant class developed a number of art forms that later became integrated into Japanese culture. Their dance and art were more dramatic and erotic than the elegant forms created by the nobility. Kabuki theater features music, dance, and extravagant costumes. Kabuki actors train from childhood and are considered to be big stars in Japan, even today. Bunraku is a form of puppet theater that uses large, nearly life-sized puppets.

The merchant class also popularized female geishas, or artistic entertainers. The art of being a geisha involves learning about music, dance, and the arts, as well as fashion and makeup. The training takes

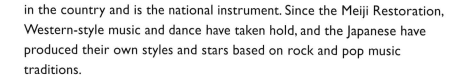

A troupe of actors performs a kabuki play.

many years. Geishas are hired to entertain guests at parties or banquets and are renowned for their grace and elegance.

Contemporary Japanese music is highly influenced by Western styles, including rock and jazz. A form of contemporary music called Japan pop, or J-pop, is very popular among adolescents and is usually performed by teenage girls.

While Western styles have also influenced dance in Japan, a striking new form of contemporary dance has been performed in recent decades. Initiated in 1959 by Hijikata Tatsumi, *butoh* is a uniquely Japanese contemporary dance. It is generally performed naked or partially naked and uses spare and elemental movements to express deep emotions.

The lyrics of the Japanese national anthem are the oldest anthem lyrics in the world.

FILM AND LITERATURE

Japan has a long tradition of literature that dates back to the sixth century and includes novels, poetry, diaries, and other written forms. The body of Japanese literature is as long and distinctive as that of English literature. It includes what is thought to be the world's first novel, *The Tale of Genji*, written by Lady Murasaki during the Heian Golden Age in the late tenth century CE. History books, accounts of court life, and poetry also date back more than 1,000 years in Japan.

It is not uncommon for the typical Japanese person to write poetry, and poems are published in newspapers and magazines. Classical Japanese poetry, influenced by the clean and simple aesthetics of Zen Buddhism and Shintoism, requires the writer to distill an image or thought in the shortest and most beautiful way. Forms of Japanese poetry include haiku, senryu, and renga.

In contemporary times, the Japanese literary tradition has continued to flourish. Among the celebrated Japanese novelists is Kawabata Yasunari, who won the Nobel Prize for Literature in 1968 and whose style of fiction draws on the simplicity and detail of Japanese poetry. More recently, novelist Murakami Haruki has captured the world's attention with his dreamlike narratives.

Since Japan's interaction with the West, movies have become popular. Perhaps the most famous Japanese filmmaker worldwide is Akira Kurosawa, who won the Golden Lion at the 1951 Venice Film Festival for *Rashomon*. Kurosawa continued to make films and won worldwide acclaim again for *Kagemusha* in 1980 and *Ran* in 1985. Other important Japanese filmmakers include Imamura Shohei, the only Japanese director to be a two-time winner of the prestigious Palme d'Or Prize at the Cannes Film Festival, and Ozu Yasujiro, director of *Tokyo Story*.

Japan has become a world leader in the field of animation. *Anime* is the word used to designate animation in Japan, and anime films embrace a wide range of subjects and styles. Miyazaki Hayao, the director of many much-loved anime films, founded his own animation studio, Ghibli. Japanese manga comics are also popular internationally.

PAPER DOORS AND GLASS SKYSCRAPERS

The national culture of Japan and the country's geologic instability have both influenced Japanese architecture. Japanese buildings were traditionally made of wood and built to withstand earthquakes and the summer heat. Designed with simple beauty, these buildings were post-and-beam structures that featured sliding mulberry paper doors and mud-packed enclosures for storing valuables.

Classical Japanese buildings include temples and castles. Since many of these were destroyed in earthquakes and wars, the vast majority have been rebuilt in the same style but with modern materials. Given this, the buildings somewhat resemble film sets.

Today, construction is a big industry in Japan. Most buildings are not more than a few decades old. Contemporary cityscapes feature glittering skylines of high-rise buildings and colorful neon signs. In recent years, some Japanese architects have constructed buildings based on traditional Japanese designs but built out of contemporary materials, such as glass and concrete. Architect Ban Shigeru is known internationally for sustainable architecture. His buildings are made from materials such as recycled cardboard and paper.

Interior of a traditional Japanese house

CHAPTER 7
POLITICS: THE EMPEROR AND THE PARLIAMENT

Japan has been a major world power for many years. During the late nineteenth and early twentieth centuries, its military might and drive to expand made it a powerful nation. Since World War II, it has been a major worldwide economic power.

Japan is an important economic and cultural force. It has diplomatic relations with nearly every nation in the world. It has belonged to the United Nations (UN) since 1956, and it is the UN's second-largest financial contributor behind the United States.[1] Japan also contributes the second-largest amount of developmental aid to nations around the world.

Japan is a member of the G8, a group of the most powerful nations in the world, and of the Asia Pacific Economic Corporation (APEC).

Emperor Akihito and Empress Michiko

For the 2009–2010 term, Japan held a nonpermanent seat on the UN Security Council. Japan is still engaged in territorial disputes with Russia, South Korea, China, and Taiwan from its expansionist era prior to World War II. However, Japan has improved relations with China since signing a friendship treaty in 1978, and it has opened economic relations with Taiwan. Despite the US occupation of Japan after World War II, Japan's key ally today is the United States.

A CONSTITUTIONAL MONARCHY

Japan's first constitution dates back to 1885, making Japan the first Asian nation to draft a constitution and institute a parliamentary style of government. A modern parliamentary government includes an elected legislature and often has a symbolic head of state, such as a monarch, who is separate from the leader of the government, usually called the prime minister. Despite the constitution and parliament, the government of the Meiji Restoration was still actively ruled by the emperor.

Japan has 100 million Internet users, the third most in the world.

Japan's current constitution was drafted by the US administration that controlled the nation for a short time after World War II. It dates back to May 3, 1947. The constitution established a parliamentary government with a constitutional monarchy. At that time, the government officially designated the emperor's power as deriving not from a divine power but from the people.

The Japan Self-Defense Forces demonstrate a military maneuver, August 28, 2010.

One unique and controversial aspect of Japan's constitution is Article 9, known as the no-war policy. The two parts of this article state first that the Japanese people "forever renounce war as a sovereign right of the nation and the threat or use of force as a means of settling international disputes" and second that "land, sea, and air forces, as well as other war potential will never be maintained."[2] Japan does maintain

ARTICLE 9

Despite the no-war clause in Article 9 of the Japanese Constitution, the nation has built up sophisticated military forces. Starting in the late 1980s, Japan began to increase the budget for the JSDF by about 5 percent each year, so that by 1990, it had the third-largest expense for defense in the world, after the Soviet Union (now Russia) and the United States.[3] Yet today, Article 9 remains in place and is widely supported by the population.

a group of military forces known as the Japan Self-Defense Forces (JSDF), which would defend the country in the event of an attack. The JSDF also sends forces to participate in UN peacekeeping actions around the world.

The royal line of the emperor has continued unbroken since the Heian Golden Age, but at different times, the emperor's power has been more ceremonial and cultural than political. Today, the emperor is the symbolic head of the nation. The political head of the government is the prime minister, who is supported by a cabinet with up to 17 members.

The parliament, called the National Diet, is made up of two chambers: the 480-member House of Representatives and the 242-member House of Councillors. The people of Japan elect the Diet. All Japanese citizens over the age of 20 are eligible to vote for these elected officials. Members of the House of Representatives elect the prime minister from among their members. The emperor then appoints the prime minister these legislators have selected. The prime minister organizes a cabinet to carry out executive duties. The House of Representatives approves the cabinet members.

Japan is divided into 47 prefectures, each of which is divided into a number of smaller subprefectures. Each prefecture is overseen by its own governor and legislature. These prefectures have less independence than US states do.

STRUCTURE OF THE GOVERNMENT OF JAPAN

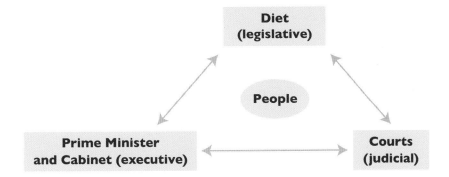

The Japanese judicial system consists of three levels of lower courts. Above the lower courts is the Supreme Court, consisting of 14 judges and a chief justice. Trials begin in local courts, but decisions can be appealed in higher courts all the way up to the Supreme Court. Japanese

The Japanese Diet meets in this building in Tokyo.

courts do not have juries, so cases are decided by the judges. Japanese law is based on a series of legal codes and on the Bill of Rights in the Constitution.

CURRENT LEADERS

Emperor Akihito took the throne on January 7, 1989, upon the death of his father, Emperor Hirohito. Akihito is the one hundred twenty-fifth emperor in a 2,000-year-old line of hereditary succession. Emperor Akihito was born December 23, 1933, and is the oldest son and fifth child of Emperor Hirohito and Empress Nagako.

As of 2011, the prime minister was Kan Naoto. He took office on June 4, 2010. Facing popular displeasure over the economy and his government's response to the March 11 earthquake, Kan promised to step down as soon as the worst of the crisis had passed. The summer of 2011 saw several candidates begin to vie for the position.

A ROYAL WEDDING

The current emperor of Japan, Emperor Akihito, was the first emperor to marry outside the royal line. When Akihito, then crown prince, married Shoda Michiko on April 10, 1959, she became the first commoner, or person not of royal blood, to become crown princess and then empress of Japan.

Michiko is the eldest daughter of Shoda Hidesaburo, the president and later honorary chairman of Nisshin Flour Milling Company. Upon the coronation of Emperor Akihito, she became Empress Michiko. The royal couple has three children: Crown Prince Naruhito, Prince Akishino, and Princess Nori.

Kan Naoto became prime minister on June 4, 2010.

The cabinet, appointed by the prime minister, can vary in size. Generally, it is composed of the Office of the Prime Minister, the Cabinet Secretariat, the Cabinet Legislative Bureau, and the National Defense Council. Power is further divided into Ministries of Education, Finance, Transportation, Agriculture, and other areas of national and international interest.

The leading political party in Japan for many years has been the Democratic Party of Japan (DPJ). This party has ruled almost every year since 1955. Other major parties include the Japan Communist Party (JCP), Liberal Democratic Party (LDP), the New Clean Government Party (Komeito), People's New Party (PNP), Social Democratic Party (SDP), and Your Party (YP).

RESILIENCE, FLEXIBILITY, AND DETERMINATION

Centuries of alternating isolationism and expansionism have allowed Japan to maintain its unique culture while benefiting from new ideas and possibilities. This process began during the third through the eighth centuries, when Japan looked to China for inspiration in organizing its government. In the nineteenth century, Japan

A SAFE COUNTRY

Japan has one of the lowest crime rates in the world. This is attributed both to the nation's strong police force and to the Japanese character, which emphasizes fitting in with family and society and respecting authority. The police force consists of the National Police Agency (NPA) and Prefectural Police (PP) and includes approximately one police officer for every 556 people in Japan.[4]

Murder is much less common in Japan than in other developed nations, including the United States. In the 20-year period from 1985 to 2004, the number of murders in Japan steadily decreased.[5] According to the NPA, there were 1,097 murders in Japan in 2009—200 less than in the previous year and one-third of the number committed in Japan in 1954, more than 50 years ago.[6] Possession of guns and other firearms is not permitted under Japanese law. Other types of crime are also decreasing, making Japan one of the safest nations on Earth.

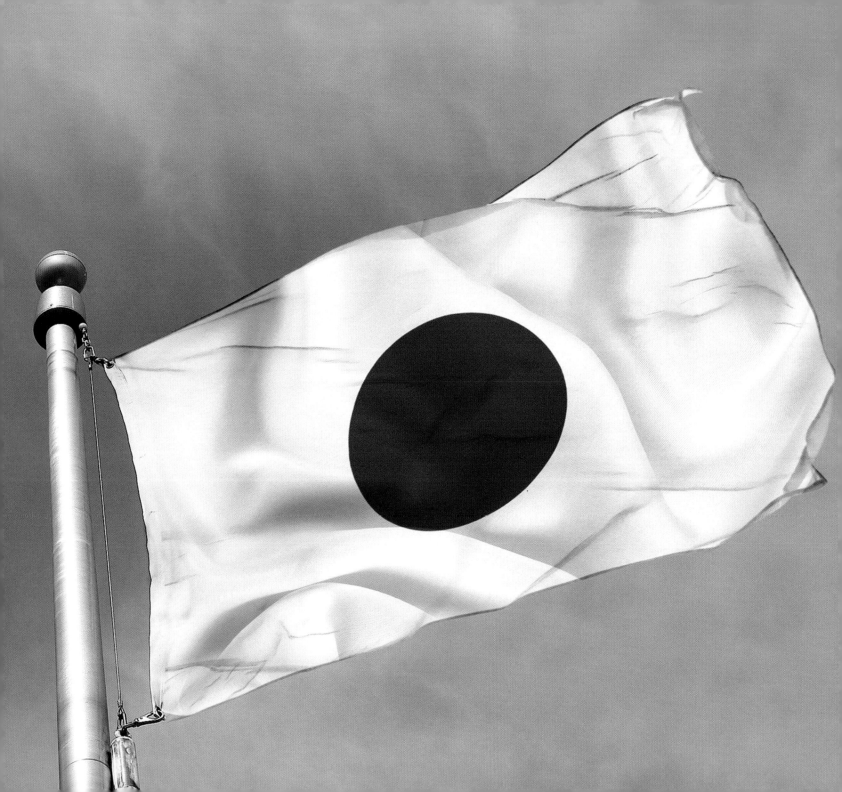

looked to the West, and its first constitution was based on European parliamentary governments. However, each time Japan has looked to other nations, it has taken the ideas and made them its own. The current government, initially organized during the brief US occupation of Japan, draws on the US Constitution but remains integrated with Japan's long history of monarchy. The emperor is still a symbolic figure in Japan, serving as both a ceremonial and cultural figurehead.

The primary strengths of the Japanese government seem to derive from its history as an island nation. Given its relative isolation and high levels of geologic activity, the Japanese have developed resiliency and flexibility. Rather than be stuck by tradition, Japan has willingly looked outside its borders to change and adapt in order to grow. More recently, change was forced on the nation by the end of World War II and US occupation. Japan adapted well to the new situation, however, learning from the US administration and embracing democracy, including giving women the right to vote.

The weaknesses of the Japanese government also seem based on its unique geographic situation. The nation's militaristic expansion during the early twentieth century was rooted in the practical desire to acquire more territory and resources. Though initially successful, the fierce persistence of the military against daunting odds during World War II led Japan to endure terrible bombings—particularly firebombs in Tokyo and atomic bombs in Hiroshima and Nagasaki—before surrendering.

The flag of Japan is white with a red circle in the center. The circle represents the sun.

CHAPTER 8
ECONOMICS: WORLD LEADER

Japan today is an economic, educational, and technological powerhouse. Measured by gross domestic product (GDP) adjusted for purchasing power, Japan has the fourth-largest economy in the world, after the European Union, the United States, and China.[1] This fact is impressive considering that Japan is a small nation (there are 60 nations in the world larger than Japan) and severely lacks natural resources.

Japan's successful economy can be attributed in large part to the dedication and hard work of its people and the nation's steadfast commitment to success. Since 1945, when Japan was essentially forced to disband its military, the nation has focused on economic development. Japan responded to a crushing military defeat with three decades of impressive economic growth. In 1960, the government announced the goal of doubling the national wealth over the next decade. During this

Commuters flood the streets of Tokyo.

period of high growth, it took less than seven years for personal incomes to double. On average, the economy grew 10 percent each year during the 1960s, 5 percent each year during the 1970s, and 4 percent each year during the 1980s.[2]

BED IN A BOX

Around the world, people have enjoyed fast food for a long time, but Japan seems to be the only nation to have developed a form of sleep-on-the-go. Capsule hotels are essentially boxes stacked in rows. Each capsule, or small room, is furnished with a sleeping mat and basic necessities, including a small television and radio, air conditioning, and an alarm clock. These specialized hotels are clustered around train stations and cater to Japanese businesspeople who missed the last train or who are too tired to go home for the night. The hotels can be small, with about 50 capsules, or as large as 600 capsules.

The Japanese work ethic is unparalleled. Businesspeople typically travel long distances to work, and it is not uncommon for them to work late into the night. Historically, the country has also guaranteed lifelong employment for workers, although this practice has begun to change.

After World War II, the Japanese banded together to rebuild their country, transforming villages made mostly of wood buildings into steel and concrete cities. By 1964, the nation had constructed the world's first national railway line for high-speed train travel. The opening of this railway line coincided with the Summer Olympic Games, held in Tokyo in

Japanese factories are known for their high-quality, precise manufacturing.

1964. The Shinkansen high-speed train—also known as the bullet train—connected Tokyo to cities all over Honshu and parts of Kushu, and it remains among the world's fastest trains.

THE SONY STORY

Morita Akio and Ibaku Masaru started Tokyo Telecommunications Engineering Corporation in 1946. The company got a jump start in 1953 when Morita purchased the rights to make a transistor, a device that improves electric signals, from the US company Western Electric. At the time, the transistor had been put to limited use in making radios, but it had not been widely marketed. The company used the transistor to make small, portable transistor radios. Its first worldwide success was the TR-63, a pocket-sized transistor radio introduced in 1957. In 1958, the company changed its name to Sony.

Sony followed its radio success with the world's first transistor television in 1960. A year later, in 1961, Sony became the first Japanese company to sell shares of its stock on the New York Stock Exchange. Before long, Sony saw another opportunity for growth. Cassette players were commercially available but not made for the general public. Sony made one and marketed it to newspaper reporters, calling it the Pressman.

By the late 1970s, Sony was at work on a new invention: a portable tape player with good sound quality, which would allow people to listen to music anywhere. The Sony Walkman, released in 1979, transformed the way people listened to music and became an international success.

Meanwhile, Japanese business leaders transformed the economy. Prior to the war, Japanese manufacturers were known for producing cheap goods. In restructuring the economy and renewing the drive toward growth, the Japanese focused on producing high-quality goods. They improved factories with precision instruments and machines, innovated new products, looked to inventions around the world for ideas, and set aside significant funds to purchase patents on foreign inventions. Their efforts turned many Japanese companies into household names, including Nintendo, Sony, Nikon, Mitsubishi, Toyota, Panasonic, Toshiba, and Honda.

The bullet train was the world's first high-speed train.

Another factor that contributed to Japan's economic success was the absolute cooperation among manufacturers, suppliers, and distributors. Groups called *keiretsu* worked together to ensure an integrated flow of products from manufacture to delivery.

MAKING THE MOST OF LIMITED RESOURCES

Japan has very limited natural resources, but because it is surrounded by water, it has an abundance of fish. The nation has capitalized on that fact by developing a fishing industry that produces 15 percent of the world's catch.[3] Japan also has some minerals, but its primary natural resource seems to be the intellectual and technological resourcefulness of its people.

Less than 15 percent of Japanese land is suitable for crops.[4] Even so, Japanese farmers have managed to develop an agriculture industry that produces enough rice for the nation and approximately 40 percent of the food for all of Japan, producing some of the largest crop yields in the smallest space in the world.[5] In addition to rice and fish, the agriculture sector produces sugar beets, vegetables, and fruit, as well as pork, poultry, dairy products, and eggs.

Prior to World War II, a majority of Japanese were farmers, fishermen, or merchants. Today, less than 4 percent of the population

A woman works in a rice field.

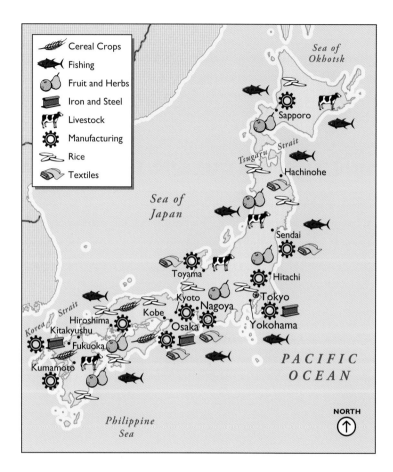

Resources of Japan

works in agriculture, and the industry receives significant cash subsidies from the Japanese government.[6] In the twenty-first century, Japan's economy is undergoing another change: shifting from an emphasis on manufacturing to an emphasis on service. As of 2011, 26.2 percent of the labor force worked in the industrial sector and 69.8 percent worked in providing services.[7]

Lacking in natural resources, Japan must import the vast majority of the fuel required for manufacturing, transportation, and other needs. In 2008, Japan was third in the world in both oil and natural gas imports.[8] In addition to fuel, imports include food, chemicals, textiles, raw materials, and machinery and equipment. Japan has one of the largest and most technologically advanced automotive industries in the world. Other successful industries include manufacturing, construction, banking, telecommunications, real estate, and retail. Japan exports transport equipment, cars, semiconductors, electric machinery, steel, electronics, and chemicals.

Tourism is another successful industry in Japan. The Japanese travel all around their beautiful nation on vacations. In addition, tourists visit Japan from all over the world to see its beautiful vistas, modern cities, and ancient shrines. Thousands climb Mount Fuji every year. Both native and foreign tourists also visit resorts in and around Japan's natural hot springs.

Most people climb Mount Fuji in July and August.

Japan's primary trading partners are the United States and China. Approximately 19 percent of exports and 22 percent of imports are traded with China, and 16 percent of exports and 11 percent of imports are traded with the United States. In addition, Japan exports to Korea, Taiwan, and Hong

Kong, and it imports from Australia, Saudi Arabia, the United Arab Emirates, South Korea, and Indonesia.[9]

LOOKING AHEAD

As of 2010, Japan's annual per capita GDP was the equivalent of $34,200, the thirty-ninth highest in the world, and the unemployment rate was approximately 5 percent.[10] Japan has long been considered an egalitarian nation with a low rate of poverty, but it has seen an increasing amount of poverty in recent years. Although Japan remains an economic leader in the world, two recessions have brought changes in some areas. Overinvestment created a financial collapse in the 1980s, when companies lost money and shed jobs. During the 1990s, growth slowed to a yearly average of 1.7 percent.[11] The economy picked up again by the first decade of the twenty-first century, just before the worldwide recession late in the decade slowed it down again.

JAPANESE CURRENCY

The official currency of Japan is the yen. One US dollar is worth approximately 80 to 90 Japanese yen. Paper money is made in values of 1,000 through 10,000 yen. Coins range from 1 to 500 yen. The yen has no smaller denominations.

Examples of Japanese yen paper money

Although Japan remains on a strong and successful economic path, it also faces challenges. The Japanese government is deeply in debt; it was estimated to owe more than 200 percent of the GDP in 2011, the highest percentage in the world.[12] The country ranks second in the world in debt, after Zimbabwe. In addition, Japan's population is both aging and shrinking in number, putting pressure on the workforce to maintain production and support those who cannot work.

The March 2011 earthquake caused several additional challenges for Japan. The country must rebuild destroyed homes and businesses and control its leaking nuclear power plants. Many of Japan's trading partners feared radiation in Japanese food, stopping exports from the entire country for a time. A 100-mile (160-km) radius around the plant is considered contaminated and food products from that area are no longer edible.

In the immediate aftermath of the quake, the Japanese stock market fluctuated rapidly. The economy stabilized, but economists estimate the cost of damage to homes and businesses at approximately $235 to $310 billion. In addition, experts fear the country's GDP may drop by as much as 1 percent in 2011.[13]

Still a dominant economic force, Japan is focusing on managing debt, improving industry and infrastructure, and making the business environment more competitive as it weathers the global recession of the first decades of the twenty-first century. Based on its past, Japan will likely find new ways to adapt and thrive in whatever the future brings.

Toyota is one of the most successful car companies in the world.

日本

CHAPTER 9
JAPAN TODAY

Daily life for most Japanese includes a blend of work and play, with leisure and recreation activities occurring after work or on the weekend. With the Japanese's renowned work ethic and tendency to let loose during free time, the expression "work hard, play hard" seems to apply to the people as a whole.

On average, the Japanese people place a high value on harmony and doing one's best. They feel significant pressure to succeed. Yet despite the Japanese emphasis on the group over the individual, Japanese people are unique individuals.

Most Japanese men devote the vast majority of their time to their employers, while women traditionally take care of children and their households. However, this has changed in recent years, as men increasingly spend time with their families and women increasingly enter and remain in the workforce.

The family is central in Japanese life.

Although hard work is a cornerstone of Japanese culture, leisure time is valued and the arts are appreciated as a regular part of life. The Japanese take part in multiple festivals involving specialized preparations. Children learn about beauty, art, and aesthetics from a young age. Young students learn origami—the art of paper folding—and study works of calligraphy and paintings. High school students take multiple courses in the arts, studying music, fine arts, crafts, and calligraphy. Many Japanese adults take courses in ikebana and practice the tea ceremony.

Few Japanese homes have ovens.

EDUCATION IN JAPAN

Japan has a highly literate population. Approximately 99 percent of Japanese aged 15 and above are able to read and write.[1] Like any form of success, this high level of literacy comes at a price. Japanese children and teens spend a significant amount of time in school. Japanese students attend school 5.5 days per week, and their average length of study is 15 years.[2] Examinations are highly competitive, and before taking tests, students often receive additional help from tutor sites called *juku*, or "cram schools."

Since 1947, the Japanese government has required children to attend elementary and middle school for a total of nine years. Beyond that,

Many Japanese schools require students to wear uniforms.

nearly all of Japan's children continue to high school, or secondary school, and about half attend a college or university, even though admission is extremely competitive.[3]

JAPANESE TEENS

In a society so dedicated to work, adolescence is considered the time to be more freewheeling and independent. Japanese teens are famous for their wild and colorful fashion sense, most famously displayed in the Harajuku district of Tokyo. These teens' distinct trends and fashions draw international attention.

HARAJUKU FASHION

Harajuku is an area in Tokyo near the train station of the same name. This area was home to the Olympic Village when the 1964 Olympic Games were held in Tokyo, and has been a popular gathering place ever since, blossoming into a stylish fashion center. The many boutiques range from high-end stores to bargain shops.

Teens and young adults there tend to favor an outrageous and vivid style that has earned the area international acclaim in the worlds of pop culture and fashion. Brightly colored hair, often fashioned into Mohawks or other modern styles, is the norm, as is clothing inspired by pop icons such as Elvis or period styles such as cowboy garb.

Some Harajuku teens test extreme styles. They earn nicknames such as Gothic Lolita, or Loli-Goth, merging Victorian dress with gothic makeup; Ganguro, bleached blonde with bronze makeup, heavy eyeliner, and sandals and miniskirts; and Kawaii-style, or cute, with pigtails, polka dots, ruffles, or animal hoodies. Other teens dress up as popular manga characters in a style called cosplay, which is short for "costume play."

Japanese teens are known for their daring and quickly changing fashion.

Japanese teens are under significant pressure to do well in school exams, as their performance reflects on their families and will greatly affect their future. However, the teens use the free time they have to have fun. Like most US teens, they enjoy video games, electronics, music, fashion, and spending time together. They are particularly interested in the latest trends in clothes, electronics, gadgets, and more. Some trends last mere weeks before being replaced by new ones.

Traditionally, slippers, not shoes, are worn in Japanese houses.

BENEFITS AND CHALLENGES

Japan will be challenged to continue its striking economic success. The strength of the labor force has been decreased by the aging population. If the low birth rate continues, the population will not replenish to maintain its numbers. A related challenge is the environment. Japan has made significant progress, internally and internationally, to protect the environment, but it also continues to face serious environmental issues caused by industrialization. In addition, the country must rebuild homes and businesses in the wake of the March 2011 earthquake.

Although Japan's traditions remain strong, the country is challenged to continue to maintain its highly developed and unique culture, even as the nation grows and reacts to change. In recent years, first Western

Japan's harmonious mix of old and new will continue to guide it into the future.

television and movies and then Internet have challenged Japan's traditional culture more than ever. While tea ceremonies, calligraphy, and Shinto rituals are still common throughout Japan, people are increasingly fascinated with the newest technology and cutting-edge fashion.

KYOTO PROTOCOL

In 1997, Japan signed an international treaty with 37 other nations to prevent global warming. The Kyoto Protocol, named for the city in Japan where it began, established limits on the amount of greenhouse gases each country could emit.[4] Greenhouse gases trap heat in Earth's atmosphere, contributing to the greenhouse effect and causing the planet's temperatures to rise.

The outlook for continued success for Japan is bright. This ancient island nation has undergone numerous international battles, only to spring back each time with a new and powerful form of development and growth. This was made most evident in the nation's dedication to technology and industry after a crushing defeat in World War II and the intense economic growth that followed. Despite new technology, Japan has remained dedicated to its unique and special culture over the centuries. Shrines and temples exist alongside factories and high-rise buildings, and the Japanese still don traditional clothing for ceremonies. The strengths of the Japanese people—acceptance of change, hard work, and dedication to the group—will continue to propel the country forward through new challenges and into new opportunities.

Japan's skyscrapers are emblems of its modernity and desire to strive for the future.

TIMELINE

13,000 BCE	By this year, Jomon people, ancestors of the present-day indigenous Ainu people, are living in Japan.
330 BCE	The Yayoi people being to arrive in Japan from Korea or China, bringing wet rice-farming techniques and metal tools.
200s CE	Queen Himiko rules over the area known as Yamato, comprised of approximately 100 kingdoms.
645	Japan is organized under a central government with a system of laws inspired by China.
712	Japan's oldest history book, *Kojiki*, is completed.
800s–1100s	The arts flourish during the Heian Golden Age.
1192	Minamoto Yoritomo establishes the Kamakura shogunate.
1199	After shogun Minamoto dies, his wife, Masako, takes power and establishes the Hojo shogunate.
1333	General Ashikaga overruns the Hojo leader and establishes the Ashikaga shogunate.
1543	Europeans arrive in Japan, beginning with shipwrecked Portuguese sailors.
1603	The Tokugawa shogunate and a period of isolation begin; the capital is moved to Edo.
1635	Most foreign commerce is banned. All Westerners except the Dutch are banned from Japan.

1853	US Naval Commodore Matthew Perry arrives in Edo Bay and soon forces the shogunate into a trade treaty.
1868	The Meiji Restoration begins; the city of Edo is renamed Tokyo.
1885	Japan drafts its first modern constitution, becoming the first Asian country to do so.
1941	On December 7, Japan attacks the US naval base at Pearl Harbor in Hawaii, prompting the United States to enter World War II.
1945	On August 6, the United States drops the world's first atomic bomb on Hiroshima, killing 90,000.
1945	On August 9, the United States drops a second atomic bomb on Nagasaki, killing nearly 40,000.
1945	On September 2, Emperor Hirohito surrenders, and the United States begins occupation of Japan.
1947	On May 3, Japan's current constitution takes effect.
1964	Japan hosts the Summer Olympic Games in Tokyo; the first bullet train in the world begins operations.
1989	Emperor Hirohito dies, and the new emperor, Akihito, takes over.
1997	The Kyoto Protocol, an international treaty for climate change, is signed in Japan.
2011	A 9.0-magnitude earthquake strikes Japan on March 11.

FACTS AT YOUR FINGERTIPS

GEOGRAPHY

Official name: Japan (in Japanese, Nihon or Nippon)

Area: 145,914 square miles (377,915 sq km)

Climate: Cool with cold winters in Hokkaido, temperate in Honshu, Shikoku, and Kyushu, subtropical in the Ryukyu Islands.

Highest elevation: Mount Fuji, 12,388 feet (3,776 m) above sea level

Lowest elevation: Lake Hachiro-gata, 13 feet (4 m) below sea level

Significant geographic features: Mount Fuji

PEOPLE

Population (July 2011 est.): 126,475,664

Most populous city: Tokyo

Ethnic groups: Japanese, 98.5 percent; Korean, 0.5 percent; Chinese, 0.4 percent; other, 0.6 percent (including Ainu)

Percentage of residents living in urban areas: 67 percent

Life expectancy: 82.25 years at birth (world rank: 5)

Language: Japanese

Religion(s): Shintoism, 83.9 percent; Buddhism, 71.4 percent; Christianity, 2 percent; other, 7.8 percent (total is greater than 100 percent because many people practice Shintoism and Buddhism.)

GOVERNMENT AND ECONOMY

Government: federal republic

Capital: Tokyo

Date of adoption of current constitution: May 3, 1947

Head of state: emperor

Head of government: prime minister

Legislature: National Diet, consists of the House of Councillors and the House of Representatives

Currency: yen

Industries and natural resources: Fish. Japan has few natural resources and must import raw materials and fuel to meet many of its industrial needs. Japan exports automobiles, steel, and electronics.

NATIONAL SYMBOLS

Holidays: A national holiday on May 3 celebrates the signing of the current constitution. The emperor's birthday, December 23, is also a national holiday.

Flag: A white rectangle with a red circle in the center

National anthem: "Kimigayo"

National animal: None; red-headed crane is an unofficial symbol

KEY PEOPLE

Queen Himiko (third century), initiated royal line of emperors

Emperor Hirohito (April 29, 1901– January 7, 1989), longest-serving Japanese emperor, led the nation during World War II

PREFECTURES OF JAPAN

Prefecture; Capital

Aichi; Nagoya

Akita; Akita

Aomori; Aomori

Chiba; Chiba

Ehime; Matsuyama

Fukui; Fukui

Fukuoka; Fukuoka

Fukushima; Fukushima

Gifu; Gifu

Gunma; Maebashi

Hiroshima; Hiroshima

Hokkaido; Sapporo

Hyogo; Kobe

Ibaraki; Mito

Ishikawa; Kanazawa

Iwate; Morioka

Kagawa; Takamatsu

Kagoshima; Kagoshima

Kanagawa; Yokohama

Kochi; Kochi

Kumamoto; Kumamoto

Kyoto; Kyoto

Mie; Tsu

Miyagi; Sendai

Miyazaki; Miyazaki

Nagano; Nagano

Nagasaki; Nagasaki

Nara; Nara

Niigata; Niigata

Oita; Oita

Okayama; Okayama

Okinawa; Naha

Osaka; Osaka

Saga; Saga

Saitama; Saitama

Shiga; Otsu

Shimane; Matsue

Shizuoka; Shizuoka

Tochigi; Utsunomiya

Tokushima; Tokushima

Tokyo (metropolis); Tokyo

Tottori; Tottori

Toyama; Toyama

Wakayama; Wakayama

Yamagata; Yamagata

Yamaguchi; Yamaguchi

Yamanashi; Kofu

GLOSSARY

aesthetics

Ideas about the nature of beauty and the appreciation of art and beauty.

Ainu

People of an ethnicity indigenous to Japan who resemble Caucasians from Russia.

austere

Having a simple or plain style, without ornamentation.

endemic

Native to a region, area, or group of people.

geothermal

Related to the heat produced by the hot interior core of the earth.

gross domestic product

A measure of a country's economy; the total of all goods and services produced in a country in a year.

ikebana

The Japanese art of flower arranging, emphasizing form and harmonious balance.

indigenous

Coming originally or naturally from an area.

kimono

A long garment with wide sleeves traditionally worn by Japanese women and men; women's kimonos are wrapped with a wide sash called an obi.

patriarchal

Controlled by men or fathers.

recession

A period in which the economy slows or shrinks.

secular

Nonreligious.

subsidies

Payments made by a government to support private companies or enterprises.

sustainable

Capable of being continued.

tectonic plates

The huge pieces that make up Earth's crust; the way plates move against each other causes earthquakes and geologic instability.

tsunami

A giant wave caused by the movement of the earth that can be destructive if it hits land.

typhoon

Large, hurricane-like storms common in Japan and other areas of the Pacific.

ADDITIONAL RESOURCES

SELECTED BIBLIOGRAPHY

"Background Note: Japan." *US Department of State*. US Department of State, 6 Oct. 2010. Web.

Rowthorn, Chris. *Lonely Planet Japan*. Victoria, Austral.: Lonely Planet, 2009. Print.

Thiro, Rosalyn. *Eyewitness Travel: Japan*. London: DK, 2009. Print.

"The World Factbook: Japan." *Central Intelligence Agency*. Central Intelligence Agency, 26 May. 2011. Web.

FURTHER READINGS

Somervill, Barbara. *Samurai, Shoguns, and Soldiers: The Rise of the Japanese Military*. Detroit, MI: Lucent, 2008. Print.

Yasuda, Yuri. *Treasury of Japanese Folktales*. North Clarendon, VT: Tuttle, 2010. Print.

Yasunari Kawabata. *Snow Country*. New York: Vintage International, 1995. Print.

WEB LINKS

To learn more about Japan, visit ABDO Publishing Company online at **www.abdopublishing.com**. Web sites about Japan are featured on our Book Links page. These links are routinely monitored and updated to provide the most current information available.

PLACES TO VISIT

If you are ever in Japan, consider checking out these important and interesting sites!

Hiroshima National Peace Memorial

This park complex includes a memorial to the victims of the Hiroshima bombing and a museum explaining the events that led up to the bombing.

Ise-jingu

This is the most sacred Shinto shrine in Japan; according to religious law, it has been rebuilt every 20 years since the third century.

Todai-Ji

This huge temple complex in Nara is the largest wooden building in the world. Daibutsu, the name of the Buddha inside, is the world's biggest indoor Buddha.

SOURCE NOTES

CHAPTER 1. A VISIT TO JAPAN

1. Rosalyn Thiro. *Eyewitness Travel: Japan*. London, New York: DK Books, 2009. Print. 93.

2. "Tokyo Tower Data." *Tokyo Tower: The Best City Landmark*. Tokyo Tower, n.d. Web. 14 Jan. 2011.

3. Ibid.

CHAPTER 2. GEOGRAPHY: AN ISLAND NATION

1. "Japan." *Encyclopædia Britannica*. Encyclopædia Britannica, 2011. Web. 14 Jan. 2011.

2. Chris Rowthorn. *Lonely Planet Japan*. Victoria, Austral.: Lonely Planet, 2009. Print. 97.

3. "The 1923 Tokyo Earthquake." *St. Louis University Earthquake Center*. St. Louis University, 1999. Web. 27 Jan. 2011.

4. Chris Rowthorn. *Lonely Planet Japan*. Victoria, Austral.: Lonely Planet, 2009. Print. 98.

5. "The World Factbook: Japan." *Central Intelligence Agency*. Central Intelligence Agency, 26 May 2011. Web. 7 June 2011.

6. "Country Guide: Japan." *BBC: Weather*. BBC, n.d. Web. 14 Jan. 2011.

7. "Background Note: Japan." *US Department of State*. US Department of State, 6 Oct. 2010. Web. 27 Jan. 2011.

CHAPTER 3. ANIMALS AND NATURE: AN ENVIRONMENT AT RISK

1. "Japan: Unique Biodiversity." *Conservation International*. Conservation International, 2010. Web. 14 Jan. 2011.

2. Conservation International. "Biological Diversity in Japan." *Encyclopedia of Earth*. Encyclopedia of Earth, 22 Aug. 2008. Web. 14 Jan. 2011.

3. "Japan: Unique Biodiversity." *Conservation International*. Conservation International, 2010. Web. 14 Jan. 2011.

4. Ibid.

5. Ibid.

6. Chris Rowthorn. *Lonely Planet Japan*. Victoria, Austral.: Lonely Planet, 2009. Print. 99.

7. Ibid. 98.

8. "Summary Statistics: Summaries by Country, Table 5, Threatened Species in Each Country." *IUCN Red List of Threatened Species.* International Union for Conservation of Nature and Natural Resources, 2010. Web. 18 Jan. 2011.

9. Ibid.

10. Chris Rowthorn. *Lonely Planet Japan.* Victoria, Austral.: Lonely Planet, 2009. Print. 100.

CHAPTER 4. HISTORY: A LEGACY OF ADAPTATION

1. Chris Rowthorn. *Lonely Planet Japan.* Victoria, Austral.: Lonely Planet, 2009. Print. 49.

2. Sidney Shalett. "First Atomic Bomb Dropped on Japan; Missile Is Equal to 20,000 Tons of TNT; Truman Warns Foe of a 'Rain of Ruin.'" *New York Times on the Web Learning Network: On This Day.* 6 Aug. 1945. New York Times, 2010. Web. 14 Jan. 2011.

3. Chris Rowthorn. *Lonely Planet Japan.* Victoria, Austral.: Lonely Planet, 2009. Print. 52.

4. "Hiroshima, Nagasaki, and Subsequent Weapons Testing." *World Nuclear Association.* World Nuclear Association, May 2010. Web. 14 Jan. 2011.

5. "Japan—Earthquake, Tsunami, and Nuclear Crisis (2011)." *New York Times.* New York Times, 7 June 2011. Web. 7 June 2011.

CHAPTER 5. PEOPLE: TRADITIONAL LIVING

1. "The World Factbook: Japan." *Central Intelligence Agency.* Central Intelligence Agency, 26 May. 2010. Web. 7 June. 2011.

2. Shigeru Miyagawa. "The Japanese Language." *Massachusetts Institute of Technology.* Massachusetts Institute of Technology, 1999. Web. 14 Jan. 2011.

3. "The World Factbook: Japan." *Central Intelligence Agency.* Central Intelligence Agency, 26 May 2011. Web. 7 June 2011.

4. Kazuyo Sawa. "Japan's Foreign Population Drops for First Time in 48 Years." *Bloomberg Business Week.* Bloomberg, 7 July 2010. Web. 27 Jan. 2011.

5. "The World Factbook: Japan." *Central Intelligence Agency.* Central Intelligence Agency, 26 May 2011. Web. 7 June 2011.

6. Chris Rowthorn. *Lonely Planet Japan.* Victoria, Austral.: Lonely Planet, 2009. Print. 59.

7. "The World Factbook: Japan." *Central Intelligence Agency*. Central Intelligence Agency, 26 May 2011. Web. 7 June 2011.

8. "Shinto." *Encyclopædia Britannica*. Encyclopædia Britannica, 2011. Web. 14 Jan. 2011.

CHAPTER 6. CULTURE: AESTHETICS AND INNOVATION

None.

CHAPTER 7. POLITICS: THE EMPEROR AND THE PARLIAMENT

1. "Background Note: Japan." *US Department of State*. US Department of State, 6 Oct. 2010. Web. 27 Jan. 2011.

2. Ronald E. Dolan and Robert L. Worden, eds. "The Article 9 'No War' Clause." *Japan: A Country Study*. Washington: GPO, 1994. Web. 14 Jan. 2011.

3. Ibid.

4. "National Police Agency." *GlobalSecurity.org*. GlobalSecurity.org, 2005. Web. 14 Jan. 2011.

5. Gavin Blair. "Murder in Japan: Killings Are Down. So Why Is Anxiety Up?" *Global Post*. Global Post, 8 Mar. 2010. Web. 14 Jan. 2011.

6. Ibid.

CHAPTER 8. ECONOMICS: WORLD LEADER

1. "The World Factbook: Japan." *Central Intelligence Agency*. Central Intelligence Agency, 26 May 2010. Web. 7 June 2011.

2. Ibid.

3. Ibid.

4. "Background Note: Japan." *US Department of State*. US Department of State, 6 Oct. 2010. Web. 27 Jan. 2011.

5. "The World Factbook: Japan." *Central Intelligence Agency*. Central Intelligence Agency, 26 May 2011. Web. 7 June 2011.

6. Ibid.

7. Ibid.

8. Ibid.

9. Ibid.

10. Ibid.

11. Ibid.

12. Ibid.

13. Ibid.

CHAPTER 9. JAPAN TODAY

1. "The World Factbook: Japan." *Central Intelligence Agency*. Central Intelligence Agency, 26 May 2011. Web. 7 June 2011.

2. Ibid.

3. "Japan's Education at a Glance, 2005." *Ministry of Education, Culture, Sports, Science, and Technology [Japan]*. Ministry of Education, Culture, Sports, Science, and Technology [Japan], 2005. Web. 14 Jan. 2011.

4. "Kyoto Protocol." *UNFCCC*. United Nations Framework Convention on Climate Change, n.d. Web. 14 Jan. 2011.

INDEX

143

PHOTO CREDITS

Hiroshi Sato/Shutterstock Images, cover; Radu Razvan/Fotolia, 2, 13; Galina Barskaya/
Shutterstock Images, 5 (top), 14; Caitlin Mirra/Shutterstock Images, 5 (middle), 34; Kyodo/
AP Images, 5 (bottom), 78, 100; Fotolia, 6, 27, 102, 109, 125, 132; Matt Kania/Map Hero, Inc., 9,
18, 23, 67, 112; Brent Bossom/iStockphoto, 11; Hiroshi Ichikawa/Shutterstock Images, 16, 130;
Atsuo Baba/iStockphoto, 20; Ippei Naoi/iStockphoto, 24, 128; Shutterstock Images, 28, 60; JTB
Photo/Photolibrary, 31, 48; Steve Kaufman/Photolibrary, 32; iStockphoto, 38, 81, 98, 104, 118,
127; Imre Cikajlo/iStockphoto, 41; Photolibrary, 42; Klaus-Werner Friedrich/Photolibrary, 46;
Archive Photos/Getty Images, 51; Library of Congress, 53; AP Images, 54, 56, 129; Koji Sasahara/
AP Images, 59; Christian Caballero/iStockphoto, 62; Gavin Hellier/Photolibrary, 64; Huang
Yao-tsung/iStockphoto, 69; Wolfgang Heidl/Fotolia, 71; Douglas Williams/Photolibrary, 72; J.
Henning Buchholz/Shutterstock Images, 75; Vladimir Vladimirov/iStockphoto, 84; Rex Butcher/
Photolibrary, 87; Tim Fan/iStockphoto, 91; Imperial Household Agency, HO/AP Images, 92,
129; Keith Tarrier/Shutterstock Images, 95; Shizuo Kambayashi/AP Images, 107; Craig Hanson/
Fotolia, 110; Igor Kisselev/Fotolia, 114, 131; Darren Brode/Shutterstock Images, 117; Radu
Razvan/Shutterstock Images, 120, Robin Laurance/Photolibrary, 122